HITTING
THE
BOOKS
Skills for Reading, Writing, and Research

D1607277

Taking Notes and Close Reading

Meg Greve

Rourke
Educational Media

rourkeeducationalmedia.com

*Scan for Related Titles
and Teacher Resources*

Before Reading:

Building Academic Vocabulary and Background Knowledge

Before reading a book, it is important to tap into what your child or students already know about the topic. This will help them develop their vocabulary, increase their reading comprehension, and make connections across the curriculum.

1. *Look at the cover of the book. What will this book be about?*
2. *What do you already know about the topic?*
3. *Let's study the Table of Contents. What will you learn about in the book's chapters?*
4. *What would you like to learn about this topic? Do you think you might learn about it from this book? Why or why not?*
5. *Use a reading journal to write about your knowledge of this topic. Record what you already know about the topic and what you hope to learn about the topic.*
6. *Read the book.*
7. *In your reading journal, record what you learned about the topic and your response to the book.*
8. *After reading the book complete the activities below.*

Content Area Vocabulary
Read the list. What do these words mean?

compare
concept
details
lecture
margins
observations
organize
refer
related
strategies
visualize

After Reading:

Comprehension and Extension Activity

After reading the book, work on the following questions with your child or students in order to check their level of reading comprehension and content mastery.

1. *How do you take notes? (Text to self connection)*
2. *What types of texts may require close reading? (Summarize)*
3. *How can having a study buddy be beneficial? (Asking questions)*
4. *Describe how you should take notes when your teacher is giving a lecture. (Summarize)*
5 *Why is it important for you to find the right way to take notes? (Infer)*

Extension Activity

Read a couple pages from your social studies book. Now try taking notes on what you read by using the Cornell note taking method, the sticky note method, and by using visuals such as pictures and diagrams. Which note taking ability works best for you?

Table of Contents

Take Note!

Do you remember everything you hear or read for the first time? Chances are you don't. If this is true for you, there are two important **strategies** that can help you remember and understand what you are learning: note taking and close reading. Both strategies are simple to use and will help you be a success in school!

Use a style of note taking called Cornell Notes. First, write the topic along the top of a page. Then, draw a vertical line down the center making two columns. Next, write key ideas in the left side column. Take detailed notes on the right side of the line. Finally, draw another line about 7 lines up from the bottom. This is where you will write a summary of your notes.

Topic:

Key ideas: Detailed Notes:

Summary:

Taking notes when your teacher is talking can be tricky. It is easy to miss something the teacher says when you are taking notes. Follow these easy steps to keep on track during a **lecture**.

1. **Organize** a notebook. Use a spiral-bound notebook or binder that has plenty of paper. Start each day with a fresh page and the date at the top.
2. Don't try to write down everything the teacher says. Instead, write short phrases or key words you can **refer** back to after class.
3. Leave spaces and **margins** while writing. You will want to go back to your notes and add information or questions you have.
4. Circle or star information you think is important or that you do not understand.
5. Listen up when the teacher says "This is important." or "I want you to understand." Circle or underline this information.
6. Copy down anything the teacher writes on the board.
7. Ask questions during the lecture.
8. Reread your notes as soon as you can. Ask the teacher about questions you still have or information you missed.

Draw pictures or diagrams with labels to help you **visualize** an idea or **concept**.

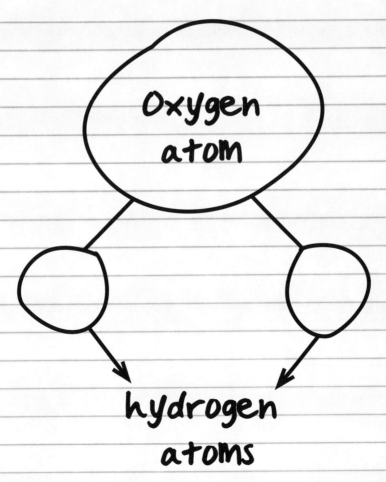

Water Molecule

Oxygen atom

hydrogen atoms

Taking notes while you are reading may seem easier than when someone is talking. But how do you know what is important and what you can leave out? You may be tempted to write down or highlight everything. This kind of note taking will only confuse you. Note taking is meant to help you remember what is really important about the concept or story. Follow these steps to help you take useful notes.

1. Organize a notebook. Use a spiral-bound notebook or binder that has plenty of paper. Write the date at the top, the title of the book, and the pages you are reading.

2. Skim the text. Look for headings, bold words, diagrams, and maps.

3. Begin reading the text carefully. Look for the main ideas and write those down. Do not copy the text. Instead, write down what you have learned in your own words.

4. Keep a list of bolded glossary words. Write down the definitions and an example of the word.

5. Write a summary of what you read after looking over your notes. If you use your own words, you are more likely to remember the information.

6. Don't forget to read the captions under pictures or illustrations. These also contain important information.

Another way to take notes while reading is by using sticky notes. Sticky notes allow you to write a note and then leave it right next to what you have read.

Whatever form of note taking you decide to use, your notes will help you understand the text when you go back to your reading. Your notes may include your own thoughts. Your notes are a good place to write down questions you have about the text. This will help you ask your teacher for help because you will be able to show exactly what you don't understand.

Study Tip

Use symbols to help organize your sticky notes. Use a question mark for something you are wondering about while reading. Use an exclamation mark when you read something really interesting. Use the letter N with a circle around it to show a new fact you have learned. Sort the sticky notes after you read to help you write a summary of your learning.

Don't Just Write the Note

You have written all of these great notes, now what? Check to see if you have notes from a previous class or reading on the same topic. Put these notes together to make a summary of your learning. The summary can be a short paragraph, a report, or even a diagram.

13

Notes are very useful when you study for a test. Use your notes to create vocabulary flashcards from your reading. Or, use them to study key ideas. Write key questions on one side of a note card and the answer on the other.

Get a study buddy and **compare** notes. Do your partner's notes have information that you missed? Copy that information onto your own notes.

Study Tip

Find any questions you wrote while taking notes. Research the correct answer or ask your study buddy or teacher.

Up Close and Reading

Have you ever finished reading an assignment and not remember anything you just read? Close reading is a strategy that can fix that problem.

Reading something more than once with a purpose in mind improves your understanding. It will help you form your own opinion on the topic. You do not have to use this strategy every time you read something. Use close reading when reading about new ideas or topics that are challenging.

Use Close Reading	Do Not Use
Science or Social Studies textbook	Entertainment magazines
Article in a newspaper	Book you are reading for fun
Book you are reading in your Language Arts class	Email from a friend
Website about a topic you are studying for a test	Website about a famous singer

When using close reading, be prepared to read the text a few times. Use note taking to help you organize your thoughts. Follow the steps below to make the most of close reading.

First Read: Read the text through. What are your first thoughts? What words do you notice first? How are they **related** to one another?

Second Read: Think of some important questions you can ask about the text. For example, what do you think the author wants you to know? How does the author write so that you can understand better?

Third Read: Think about what your teacher is asking about the text. Are you making any connections between yourself and the text, or another piece of reading?

Do not take too many notes during your first read. Think about the main idea the author is trying to make.

Magnificent Magnifiers

When you are using close reading, ask yourself questions about the text while you read. By asking questions, you will be more likely to find clues to the answers as you continue to read.

Use the following questions to guide your understanding and form your own **observations** about the text.

- What are some important words you are reading? How do they relate to the topic?
- Do you notice any patterns the author uses?
- How do you feel about the character or topic? What is it about the passage that makes you feel this way?
- Is there information that you think might be missing? What is it? Why do you think this is important?
- Is there a message or main idea? What **details** lead you to this idea?

Practice note taking and close reading on your own. You can download short articles from popular websites or use books from the library. Both strategies will lead you to a better and deeper understanding. Success is just a note away!

Glossary

compare (kum-PAYR): notice what is the same or different

concept (KON-sept): an idea

details (di-TAYLS): smaller ideas that make up one big idea

lecture (LEK-chur): a talk meant to teach others about something

margins (MAR-juhns): spaces along the sides of paper

observations (ob-zur-VAY-shuhns): things you have noticed about something

organize (OR-gan-ize): put everything in a neat and ordered way

refer (ri-FUR): look back at something

related (ri-LAY-tid): being connected

strategies (STRAT-uh-jees): smart plans to meet a goal or solve a problem

visualize (VIZH-oo-uh-lize): see something in your mind

Index

Websites to Visit

ezinearticles.com/?Teaching-Kids-To-Take-Notes-For-School&id=5436069

www.how-to-study.com/study-skills-articles/taking-notes-in-class.asp

kids.nationalgeographic.com/kids/

About the Author

Meg Greve lives in Chicago with her husband Tom, and her two children, Madison and William. They are always working hard to be successful in school and out of school!

Meet The Author!
www.meetREMauthors.com

www.rourkeeducationalmedia.com

PHOTO CREDITS: Cover © Alejandro Rivera; title page © africa-studio.com; page 3 © DNY59; page 4 © monkeybusinessimages; page 5, 7, 11, 15 © kmitu, sak12344; page 8 © Gravicapa; page 10 © Antonio Guillem; page 12 © Syda productions, page 13 © Cathy Yeulet; page 14 © SusaZoom; page 15 © Odua; page 16 © racorn; page 18 © CEFutcher; page 22 © Ryan Dashinsky

Edited by: Jill Sherman

Cover Design by: Tara Raymo

Interior Design by: Jen Thomas

Library of Congress PCN Data

Taking Notes and Close Reading / Meg Greve
(Hitting the Books: Skills for Reading, Writing, and Research)
ISBN (hard cover) (alk. paper) 978-1-62717-689-7
ISBN (soft cover) 978-1-62717-811-2
ISBN (e-Book) 978-1-62717-926-3
Library of Congress Control Number: 2014935483

Rourke Educational Media
Printed in the United States of America,
North Mankato, Minnesota

Also Available as: